INTRODUCTION

2.00

£ 3.00

T0081263

'Simplicia' is the story of a naive youn[g]
courageous freedom fighter and potential[ ]
set sometime during the late 'Dark Age'/
the background of war, somewhere in Euro[pe]
historical accuracy as the main aim of t[he]
moral play with allegorical overtones.

The songs, designed to be sung by young voices, are contemporary in style and essential to the telling of the story.

The Christian background of the play is designed to provide a suitable ideology for the normally passive 'Patriots' and a motivation for Simplicia.

The production is intended for use by either a secondary or middle school and the script has been designed for use on an average school stage, though the Haggerston production extended the stage by using rostra, leaving a gap in the middle for the band. Its production relies on a large cast rather than costly sets and expensive costumes.

Although written for a girls' school it is just as suitable for a co-educational school. One of the immediate advantages of a mixed cast is that it enables the 'Raiders' to be played by the boys, while the 'Patriots' should clearly be a mixture of both sexes. The number of major parts exclusively female are not as many as an initial glance might suggest.

Speaking parts have been kept deliberately to a minimum allowing more scope for large choirs to convey the full meaning of the songs without the stage becoming cluttered.

The part of Simplicia was originally designed to be played by two girls (the change coming at the end of Act I) but this idea was scrapped in the original production.

The following is the production script with minor modifications, which have been explained at the bottom of the appropriate page.

The duration of the production is 80-85 minutes (depending on the length of scene changes) and with a 15 minute interval becomes a useful length for a school production.

The production was possible only through the efforts of the staff and pupils of Haggerston School and it is to them that this musical is dedicated.

Tony Purcell
1980

THE STORY

Simplicia is considered by her parents to be stupid and only good
enough for guarding the family sheep from wolves. She does not know
what they look like and mistakes a raiding party of Barbarians, a
warlike neighbouring tribe who have her homeland under attack, for
wolves. Her family is attacked and killed but she manages to escape
to a nearby forest where the trees shelter her for the night. The
next morning she is discovered by an old Nun who allows Simplicia to
stay with her. Over a period of three years the old Nun teaches
Simplicia the difference between right and wrong, eventually baptising
her. Shortly afterwards the old Nun dies, her final advice to
Simplicia - "to know yourself". Simplicia leaves the forest only
to be captured by the Barbarians. The Barbarian Queen is fascinated
by her and wants her as a pet. Made a fool of by the General at a
special banquet, she is forced to don the clothes of a donkey.
Simplicia learns the art of survival but is shocked by the apparent
immorality of the Barbarians. The timely intervention of a troop of
Patriots, led by Edward, enables her to escape. The second Act opens
two years later. Simplicia has returned to the forest awaiting
inspiration from the Nun. She is captured by Edward and put on
trial as a spy. Under interrogation from Edmund, it is discovered
that the old Nun was Edmund's sister and he decides to adopt
Simplicia. Edward is given the job of teaching her to fight and
he begins to fall in love with her. Edmund is killed by the Barbarians
and the Gold Cup (Patriot symbol) is stolen. Edward and his men set
out to avenge the death of his father and retrieve the Gold Cup.
Meanwhile, Simplicia, now ironically nicknamed the Wolf, forms her
own guerilla band to harass the Barbarians. Hearing of her exploits,
Ellen, a camp follower who is tired of her treatment by the Patriot
males, decides to join Simplicia. Simplicia and her followers attack
the General's encampment. The General is forced to undergo the same
indignities he had earlier forced on Simplicia and to return the
Gold Cup. Returning to the Patriot camp Simplicia hears that Edward
has engaged the enemy and decides to lead the Patriots to relieve his
beleagued forces. A battle follows and though the Patriots win, there
are a large number of deaths including, or so Simplicia thinks, Edward.
The two armies unite to form a new State and offer Simplicia the crown.
She refuses, and goes in search of Edward hoping he is still alive.
They return united, and Simplicia becomes the leader and the mentor
of the newly formed State.

THE SONGS

ACT I

Scene 1   "The Raiders' Song" - The Raiders

Scene 2   "Morning Was So Long Ago" - Simplicia and the Trees

Scene 3   "The Nun's Song" - The Nun and Simplicia

Scene 4   "Prisoners of War" - The Patriots

Scene 5   "The Fool's Song" - Simplicia

ACT II

Scene 7   "The Patriots' Anthem" - The Patriots

Scene 8   "The Love Duet" - Edward and Simplicia

Scene 9   "The Ballad of Simplicia" - Aidan and the Patriots

Scene 10   "The General's Song" - The General

Scene 11   "Gloria" - The Patriots

            "The Patriots' Anthem" - The Patriots

Scene 12   "The Finale" - (a) The Patriots and the Barbarians

                         (b) Edward and Simplicia, the Whole Cast

                         (c) The Whole Cast

THE MUSIC

A separate publication contains the Vocal and Piano Score for the Songs
and the Incidental Music. The cues for the Music are indicated clearly
in the Libretto, but fuller details are provided in the Score. Chorus
parts are also available.
Two versions of "The Love Duet" (Nos. 18 and 18a) are contained in the
Score. The original version was written for a girl playing Edward,
while the alternate version (18a) is more suitable if a boy has the role.

TAPE CUES

The Sound Effects used in the Haggerston School production were taken
from BBC Sound Effects records, nos. RED 126M, RED 164S, REC 225,
REC 269, REC 295.
Briefly, the tapes were constructed as follows:-

Tape Cue No. 1
Sounds of battle, fading after about twenty seconds into 'early
morning' sounds of birds and wind-in-the-trees as Music Cue No. 1
begins. This tape continued through No. 1 and included three wolf
howls (referred to in the script).

Tape Cue Nos. 2 and 3

'Early morning' - birds, trees, babbling brook, etc.
Part of this tape was repeated (Tape Cue No. 3) after the line
"Help me fill that void with love for Thee, before the wolves of this
world tear her soul between their teeth".

Tape Cue No. 4

Sounds of battle, at first distant but getting closer and closer. The
entry of Edward's followers and Simplicia's retrieval of the gold all
take place with this tape still running.

Tape Cue No. 5

The 'supernatural' voice of the Nun was achieved by applying
artificial echo to an ordinary recording of the line "Find thyself
and be true Simplicia".

Tape Cue No. 6

Various 'supernatural' sound effects mixed together to accompany
Simplicia's incantation.

Tape Cue No. 7

The entire battle scene (up to the entrance of Simplicia) was
accompanied by a 'battle' sound effects tape; this was approximately
three minutes in length.

THE ORCHESTRA

In the original production, a small orchestral band, consisting of
two Flutes, two Clarinets, Clarinet doubling E flat Saxophone, Trumpet
and Trombone was used. The parts played by these instrumentalists
basically doubled the piano part and were of a relatively simple
standard. These parts are available from the publishers (and their
entries are indicated in the Vocal Score) although schools are
welcome to write extra orchestral parts if so desired.
No drummer was used in the original production. The drumming
indications in the Vocal Score (Nos. 2,3,7 and 19) were achieved with
a foot-operated Bass Drum and a Tenor Drum, both played by the pianist.
The judicious use of a drummer in other numbers might be appropriate.
The 'Ballad of Simplicia' (No. 20) was arranged so that Aidan could
accompany himself (herself) on stage using a guitar.

AMPLIFICATION

An amplification system was used in the original production for the
solo singers and for the tape-recorder. Microphones were placed on
stands at the foot of the front of the stage. The use of scaffolding
for a stage set enabled the microphones not to appear too obtrusive.

PRODUCTION NOTES

LIGHTING

Lighting is very important to the production of Simplicia for it is used to create scene changes, a variety of different settings and atmosphere. A lighting plot is not included here owing to the widely differing facilities producers will have available. Major lighting changes, where they enhance the flow and understanding of the plot, have been included in the script.

COSTUMES

Simplicia has no specific historical setting and therefore costume designers can be reasonably free in their choice of designs. Indications of costume in the script are intended as a guide to the type of costume which may be appropriate for that section of the plot or where a costume change takes place (e.g. Simplicia, Ellen). The Prisoners, if they are used as the Patriot Army in Act II, should also have a change of costume.
The cultural differences between the two opposing sides should be reflected in their costumes. Colours, unless indicated, will depend on the costume designer and producer/director.

STAGE SET

The play has been designed for a school stage, though there may be a need to extend the stage (e.g. using rostra) to accomodate the numbers. The stage set should not be elaborate as scene locations vary and scene changes need to be rapid, preferably without the use of curtains.
The original set was a configuration of scaffolding, intended to present an aura of bleakness and divide the stage into several acting areas. Rostra were used to extend the acting area with a space in the middle for the orchestra. No backdrops nor flats were used, nor were any raised acting levels. Lighting indicated a change of scene.

PROPERTIES

Props play a vital role in the production, particularly if no stage set is used. However it is necessary to keep these to a minimum. Important props are included in the stage directions of the script. This list should not be considered definitive.

CHARACTERS in order of first appearance

Characters marked * have speaking parts of more than a few words in length. Those who also sing have been indicated elsewhere in the introduction, whether as soloists or part of a chorus.

*Simplicia's father

*Simplicia's mother

*Ursula, Simplicia's sister

*Simplicia

*Leader of the Raiders (Raider 1 in script)

 Raiders (9 - 12) - at least two have lines

 Trees (8 - 12)

 Fireflies (3 - 5)

*The Nun

 Tableaux Characters (if used - see script notes)

 Patriot Prisoners (30 - 40) - later used as Patriot Army

*Barbarian King

*Barbarian Queen

*Barbarian General

 Attendants - possibly costumed stage crew (4 - 6)

 Banquet Guests (12)

*Edward, Edmund's son

*Olgard, Edward's lieutenant

 Edward's followers (3 - 4 Patriots)

*Simplicia II (if used - see introduction and script notes)

 Patriot Army (use Prisoners) - 3 have speaking parts in Scene 9

 Two Throne Guards

*Patriot Officer

*Edmund, Leader of the Patriots

*Ellen, a camp follower - later joins Simplicia

 Camp Followers (4 - 6)

 Aidan, a minstrel

 Two Barbarian Bodyguards

*General's Attendant

*Godwin, Simplicia's lieutenant

*Andrea, a follower of Simplicia

*Patriot Messenger

SIMPLICIA

ACT I

<u>TAPE CUE 1</u>*

SCENE 1   A PEASANT FARM

<u>MUSIC CUE 1</u>

*As the curtain opens the lights fade up slowly. It is dawn. On the
stage left the family rises. Simplicia's mother and her sister prepare
the morning meal. Her father rises and sits waiting for his meal. A
cock crows in the distance. This action freezes and the lights cross
to stage right.*
*Simplicia rises with bagpipes under her arm. She is tired and cold
having spent most of the night watching over sheep and goats. She
rubs her hands and huddles to keep warm. She yawns, stretches and
scans the horizon. She moves downstage rounding up the animals. She
pats them, whistles to them, talks to them. She is very close to the
animals. Upstage R. a group of 3-4 Raiders enters and quietly lurks in
the shadows. They watch Simplicia keenly. The Raiders move in slowly
during the dialogue.*

SIMPLICIA
*as she moves amongst the animals***
Come on you silly old thing...keep with the others...I'll
play my bagpipes when we get there
wolf howl
...no, not yet...come on...oh please hurry...I will be in
trouble
wolf howl
...why do you have to eat now?...I haven't eaten yet...get
moving...

*The wolf howl is heard again, closer. Simplicia stops and looks afraid.
The Raiders have moved closer.*

SIMPLICIA
to the animals
Was that an evil sound?...perhaps it was a wolf...father
told me about wolves...he said they come out of the night...
they take sheep and sometimes little girls, too...I don't
know what they look like though...I wonder how many legs
they have?...I shall blow my bagpipes as hard as I can, just
in case.

She blows very hard on her bagpipes. As she does so, the Raiders creep

*See Music Score and Introduction for all tape cues
** See Score - Music Cue 1

1

up beside her. They encircle Simplicia. She stops playing. She is
aware that there is a threat. She is not sure of its nature. The
Raiders laugh and taunt her. They give mock wolf howls and laugh at
her reaction. The Raiders and Simplicia stare at each other. Silence.

SIMPLICIA
Are you wolves?

MUSIC CUE 2

*A Raider moves slowly to Simplicia and grabs the bagpipes. Simplicia
tries to snatch them back again and almost succeeds. The bagpipes
are thrown about by the Raiders while Simplicia tries to retrieve them.
She is unsure of what is happening. Suddenly the game, with its
sinister laughter, stops. Slowly the Raiders surround Simplicia,
hissing. She backs away. The Raiders follow her menacingly, more
quickly.*

SIMPLICIA
moving backwards
All the sheep are scattered...come here, poor old Billy-
Goat...help me round them up...my father will belt me for
this...he'll belt you too...help me get them, then it will
be alright...What are you?

*The Raiders grab Simplicia and sweep offstage R. The family go about
their business using more space on stage. They are unaware of what
is happening outside until suddenly the 4 Raiders burst in and throw
Simplicia against her parents. They are joined by the remaining
Raiders who arrange themselves suitably about the stage.*

RAIDER 1
So this is your home, girl! Is your sister a pretty wench?

*He grabs her and kisses her roughly. She breaks away. The other
Raiders laugh.*

RAIDER 2
Is your mother a good cook?

RAIDER 3
Is your father a good for nothing?

*He kicks the father viciously, who then goes to retaliate but is
restrained by his wife.*

SIMPLICIA
innocently
No, I am.

*This relaxes the atmosphere a little. The leader (Raider 1) pulls
the mother aside.*

2

RAIDER 1
How about a little welcoming food?

The mother brings a bowl of food. The Raiders eat ravenously. The mother crosses herself. Simplicia busies herself passing more food. There is a lot of laughing and shouting.

RAIDER 2
Beer!

RAIDER 3
Beer!

RAIDERS
Stomping and shouting
Beer...beer...beer...

RAIDER 1
signalling them to stop
Now, men, this is a civilised Christian home. Where are your manners?
laughter
to Simplicia
Get some beer, girl.
to the mother, overpolitely
And from you some meat, my dear lady.

MOTHER
We have no meat, sir. We are poor peasants.

RAIDER 1
Now that is not a Christian attitude.
to two Raiders
See what you can find outside, boys.

The two Raiders exit. Simplicia and Ursula hand out jugs of beer. The Raiders continue to gorge and drink. The rest of the family huddles together, frightened.

RAIDER 2
in between mouthfuls
I saw a big fat pig outside.

The sound of a squealing pig, mixed with laughter, is heard offstage. The two Raiders reappear with a dead pig.

FATHER
leaping forward
Not the sow! Not the sow!

He is knocked to the ground by the Raiders. Ursula goes to help her father.

RAIDER 1
Leave him there, girl. Get some more beer.

MUSIC CUE 3   THE RAIDERS' SONG

RAIDERS
We come from the east, we are Raiders,
Hungry for the feast, we are Raiders,
Looting land is fun, we are Raiders,
Armies on the run, we are Raiders.

Bring us meat and bring us beer,
Or else we'll teach you fear, we are Raiders.

Treat us right for we are the Raiders,
Spoiling for a fight, we are Raiders,
Killing is such joy to the Raiders,
Willing to destroy, we are Raiders.

Bring us meat and bring us beer,
Or else we'll teach you fear, we are Raiders.

*During the song the mother and Ursula rescue the father. At the
end of the song the Raiders turn leeringly towards the women, but
not Simplicia.*

RAIDERS
together
Women!

MOTHER
crossing herself
God help me.

URSULA
Be merciful.

*The Raiders lunge at the two women. There is a lot of yelling and
screaming. The father tries to save his wife and is instantly killed.
One Raider grabs Ursula and drags her offstage R. Several others form
into two groups and play a 'cat and mouse game' with the mother who is
trapped between them. One group manages to catch her and drags her offstage R. The other group joins the remaining Raiders who are looting
and torching the farmhouse. Everything should be removed from the
stage including the dead father and sow. Simplicia remains huddled
in a corner unable to understand what is going on. She clutches her
bagpipes. A dishevelled Ursula rushes on stage to Simplicia.*

URSULA
frantic
Run!...Run to the forest...run!...RUN!

On the last 'run' a Raider grabs Ursula and drags her offstage R.
Shocked into action and following orders Simplicia escapes L.   The
stage is empty. Lights fade.

SCENE 2   THE FOREST OF HANAVEN

The forest is dark. At the start of this scene lights should only
silhouette the action.   The Trees enter and take up their positions.
Simplicia enters stage L. and crosses through the Trees to stage R.
(offstage).

MUSIC CUE 4

More light creating a shadowy, eerie effect.
The Trees begin their dance. Fireflies dart amongst the Trees and
as they catch the light the atmosphere should almost be ghostly. As
the dance nears its climax the Trees coax Simplicia onto the stage
and gently guide her downstage R. Frightened, cold and alone she
begins to sing. The Trees move in around her to protect her.

MUSIC CUE 5   MORNING WAS SO LONG AGO

SIMPLICIA
Morning was so long ago,
Tired and cold, my spirit's low,
Shadows all around me
Play tricks about me,
I long to be back home.

Tiny stars to light my way,
Sadly though no sheep to play,
Darkness closing round me,
And sounds that haunt me,
I'd like to sleep till day.

What am I to do here?
Where to go?
How did I arrive here?
I don't know.
Lost and all alone,
Now wolves have taken all my sheep.

Staying here all through the night,
Keeping hidden out of sight,
Waiting for the new dawn,
Returning once more,
To make the darkness bright.

Simplicia is obviously tired and during the next section of the song
she curls up and goes to sleep at the foot of the Trees using her
bagpipes, which she has brought with her, as a pillow.

5

TREES
Night has brought a gift we see,
Looks so tired, who can she be?
Who has sent her to us?
The child beneath us
Is sad but she is free.

Weeping with no place to go,
Waiting for the lights to show,
Duty means we watch her,
Protect and guard her
From danger down below.

What is she to do here?
Where to go?
How did she arrive here?
We don't know.
Lost and all alone,
Now wolves have taken all her sheep.

We will rock her fast asleep,
Shade her with our branches deep,
Gently now don't wake her,
We must not scare her;
Caress her while asleep.

At the end of the song the Trees take one last look at Simplicia and leave the stage quietly. She remains fast asleep. The lights fade.

SCENE 3   THE FOREST OF HANAVEN: THE NUN

TAPE CUE 2

It is dawn. The light of the morning breaks to a dawn chorus including a distinct sound of a blackbird. An old Nun dressed in sackcloth with a giant cross about her neck enters. She whistles to the bird, then falls on her knees. Tape fades.

NUN
praying
Glory be to God. All his works are fresh, all his gifts are precious.
She rises and notices Simplicia
Well what have we here? One of God's creatures? By the look of him he looks more like one of the devil's.

The Nun shakes Simplicia, who wakes with a start. She sees the Nun and immediately grabs for her bagpipes. She blows and the noise is horrific. The Nun backs away and crosses herself.

NUN
Mercy! It is the devil himself.

SIMPLICIA
terrified
Get away wolf! Get off! Get away you old wolf.
she drops the bagpipes

NUN
Mercy! It's a little girl.
she picks up the bagpipes. Simplicia backs away.
The devil's instrument maybe. It certainly sounds like it.

SIMPLICIA
not daring to move
Don't hurt my bagpipes.

NUN
Bagpipes are they? Here they are. I won't hurt them.
Come here and get them so we can stop talking in this
ridiculous way.

SIMPLICIA
a little reassured by the kindness in the Nun's voice
My father warned me about wolves.

NUN
A good thing too, but there are no wolves here. Come on,
take my hand. I won't hurt you. It's quite safe.

*The sight of the held out hand frightens Simplicia and she begins to
cry.*

SIMPLICIA
Get away. I know wolves. I've just escaped from wolves.
You are a wolf and you will eat me up.

NUN
I tell you there are no wolves here. I am a servant of
God - a hermit. I will not harm you. I will not eat you
...Are you hungry? I have some food back at my shelter...
Look, I'll stand back here and then you can follow me at
a safe distance.

*Simplicia begins to follow the nun tentatively but stops everytime
the Nun stops. It turns into a game for the Nun. She moves,
Simplicia moves. She stops, Simplicia stops. She runs, Simplicia
runs. They eventually reach the Nun's hut upstage L. The Nun gives
Simplicia some food. She gulps it down.*

SIMPLICIA
You're not a wolf then.
she is feeling much better

NUN
No.

SIMPLICIA
Oh!
she wipes her mouth

NUN
Have you had enough?

SIMPLICIA
Yes.

NUN
You haven't given thanks yet.

SIMPLICIA
Oh yes. Thank you.

NUN
No, not to me. To God.

SIMPLICIA
I don't know him.

NUN
You don't know God!

SIMPLICIA
No. Our nearest neighbours were ten miles away.

NUN
Have you never heard of 'The Lord's Prayer'?

SIMPLICIA
Oh yes. My mum said it sometimes.

NUN
Can you say it?

SIMPLICIA
Of course I can. I'm not stupid.
she joins her hands and bows her head mimicking her mother
"Our dear father child in heaven, hollow is thy name you
will be done on earth and in heaven, give us our daily
bread and trespass against us for fire in the kingdom the
powerful story for ever and ever and ever and ever..."

NUN
Amen.

SIMPLICIA
I was coming to that.

NUN
You must listen and learn. You are as ignorant as the
blackbird I heard this morning. You know neither yourself
nor God. You are a Simplicia in all your being.

SIMPLICIA
My father just called me 'girl' and sometimes 'good for
nothing' but Simplicia sounds better though.
she gets up to leave

NUN
Where are you going?

SIMPLICIA
I don't know. I haven't thought yet. They chased Ursula
and burnt the house and killed the sow.

NUN
putting her arm round Simplicia
Who did?

SIMPLICIA
incredulously
The wolves of course.

NUN
My daughter, you can stay here with me. You are safe here.
There's not much comfort, but all I have is yours.
Simplicia yawns
You are tired. Go inside and sleep.

*Simplicia exits stage L. The lights fade slowly throughout the next
piece of dialogue. The Nun kneels.*

NUN
Help me show this child, who has the innocence of a new
born lamb, Thy ways. Her simplicity has kept her soul
untouched by the world. Help me fill that void with love
for Thee, before the wolves of this world tear her soul
between their teeth.

TAPE CUE 3

*At the end of this prayer the lights come up again. It is a new day.
Simplicia enters and comes straight to the Nun.*

SIMPLICIA
You told me you were in the forest to find god. I've looked
for him all morning but all I found were these violets under

9

the leaves.
she hands the Nun a bunch of violets.
I did hear that bird again, though. I'll look again tomorrow,
but I don't think god's in this forest.

NUN
He's there, Simplicia. The blackbird you heard was God, **and**
the wind and the violets.

SIMPLICIA
I think I'll go back to looking after animals. That was
much easier.

NUN
Yes, this way is hard. We are only human. Listen to what
I read to you.
She picks up a Bible.

SIMPLICIA
What's that?

NUN
The Bible. A book.

Simplicia looks confused but says nothing. The Nun walks to stage R.
Instead of reading she sings. Upstage a tableau is performed
depicting the creation and downfall of Adam and Eve.* Towards the end
of this section of the song Eve comes forward and places a hessian
rope about Simplicia's waist.

<u>MUSIC CUE 6a</u>   THE NUN'S SONG

NUN
Our Lord God toiled to make the whole world right,
All was perfect in His sight,
He made Man and then He smiled,
But this man was soon beguiled,
And the beauty he defiled.

For the serpent tempted his wife,
And scattered the seeds of discord into life;
Sorrow, sickness, thistles and dust,
God's own splendour, ruined by Man's lust.

At the end of this section of the song Simplicia looks confused.
She runs back to the hut and picks up her bagpipes.

*In the original production the tableau was not performed.
The passage of time was shown by a lighting cue before the
beginning of sections b) and c) of the song.

NUN
Where are you going?

SIMPLICIA
I'm off. Is this what you are looking for? Is this what
you love? Someone who gives you thorns and thistles and
dust and sweat and sorrow!

NUN
Wait. Wait, Simplicia. God loves us all.

SIMPLICIA
Loves us! Loves us! I'd rather be loved by a wolf. My
father didn't think much of me, but he did give us bread
and a warm bed.

NUN
Simplicia, God gave Adam a choice...we all have the same
choice, just as you may choose whether to go or stay.

*Simplicia puts down the bagpipes and returns to the Nun who has moved to
stage L. The tableau returns to depict the story of Judith. Towards the
end of this section Judith steps forward and places a plaited girdle on
Simplicia.*

MUSIC CUE 6b

NUN
Judith, widow of the city of Judea,
Put off mourning, bleak and drear,
At the army drawing near,
And her people wrapped in fear,
For her purpose now was clear.

She knelt and prayed to our Lord,
To save her from cruel men who would rule the world,
Seduced their leader, left him dead;
On seeing this the mighty army fled.

Simplicia again looks confused and concerned.

SIMPLICIA
Sister, why does God let war happen?

NUN
Child, God doesn't let war happen. He has given the human
race a free choice and it is us who let it happen. We have
a choice between God and the devil, but sadly we all too
often choose the devil.

*Although Simplicia is still very innocent she is beginning to learn.
The tableau depicts the birth of Christ. At the end of the song Mary
places a crown of flowers on Simplicia's head.*

MUSIC CUE 6c

NUN
Jesus Christ was born in a cave in Bethlehem,
To be God's one hope for men.
Unto Him did angels sing,
And the wise men gifts did bring:
Hallelujah, Christ is King.

Even now His hope still shines bright,
I willingly take it for my guiding light.
Honour due, so praises sing:
Hallelujah, Christ the Lord is King.

NUN AND SIMPLICIA
Jesus Christ was born in a cave in Bethlehem,
To be God's one hope for men,
With the comfort it would bring.
So let us His praises sing:
Hallelujah, Christ is King.

*The tableau exits. The Nun hands Simplicia the Bible. She begins to
read tentatively.*

SIMPLICIA
reading
"Jesus cried with a loud voice: My God, my God, why has
thou forsaken me? Jesus, when he had cried again with a
loud voice, yielded up the ghost."
she closes the book and looks up at the Nun
Why is God so cruel, Sister? Why did He kill His only son?

NUN
He died for us, Simplicia. But remember God didn't kill Him.
Humans chose to kill Him. We still have the gift of choice.

SIMPLICIA
after thinking for a moment
It is a great love. Sister, I choose this way...Will you
baptise me?

NUN
Simplicia, I have waited patiently since your coming into
the forest, almost three years ago, for this moment.

*The Nun leads Simplicia to another part of the stage. She baptises
her. The Nun gives Simplicia the Bible. Simplicia kisses the cross.*

NUN
Now Simplicia, the time has come for me to leave this world.

SIMPLICIA
very upset
Will you leave me alone in this wild forest? Will you...

12

Simplicia is overcome and falls at the Nun's feet. The Nun picks her up and consoles her.

NUN
Don't cry, child. Follow my last words, which are 'to know yourself'. Most of us are condemned because we do not know who we have been, or what we could become. When my soul has gone to the appointed place, cover me with the earth and fallen leaves.
she clasps Simplicia
Dear child, I will die happier in the knowledge that He will protect you.

SIMPLICIA
clinging to the Nun
Please do not make me go...or leave me alone...

NUN
sternly
Simplicia, leave me.

The Nun exits stage R. Simplicia returns to the hut and collects her bagpipes then moves downstage centre.

SIMPLICIA
Dear God, please make my beloved friend return.

She begins to cry as she exits stage R. The lights fade.

SCENE 4   ANOTHER PART OF THE FOREST: A PRISONER

As the lights come up the stage is empty. Two columns of Prisoners guarded by the Raiders from scene 1 enter from both sides of the stage to a drum beat.*
As they meet in the middle the Guards salute each other in an appropriate manner. One group crosses to stage L. When they have passed, the other group crosses to stage R. The Guards let them rest and some of the Guards have a friendly chat in the centre of the stage. At this point Simplicia enters stage R. minus tableaux costume (if used) and the Bible and bagpipes. She recognises the Raiders and is about to run when she is captured and thrown to the front of the stage. The Raiders do not recognise her.

MUSIC CUE 7   PRISONERS OF WAR

PRISONERS
Pris'ners of war we are.
What are we fighting for?
They have our land, they have our men,
Will there be freedom to live again?

* see Score

13

They took our freedom away.
Is this the price we must pay?
They speak of wealth, what do they mean?
Death and destruction is all we've seen.

See your sad country, what does she mean to you?
Mean to you?
Lost yet true,
Lost to you who love her so,
Lost to you who let her go,
Yet you know we'll pull through.
We shall not rest nor fail,
Not turn aside nor pale,
Until we're home, the battle won,
So onward, on my good friends.

*At the end of the song the Prisoners and Guards on stage R. depart.
Simplicia is roughly shoved to the end of the line of Prisoners who
remain, on stage L. The lights fade.*

SCENE 5   THE BARBARIAN CAMP

*The lights come up. The Barbarian King and Queen enter stage L.
followed by the Barbarian General. They study the captives then
move to the R. of the stage.*

KING
As the war goes on, the captives get lazier...

GENERAL
...and more ragged...

QUEEN
holding her nose
...and they stink more.

GENERAL
What are you going to do with them?

KING
You deal with them.

*The General clicks his fingers and the Prisoners are led off stage.
As they pass the royal party the Queen notices Simplicia.*

QUEEN
What's that at the end of the line?

The General clicks his fingers to stop the last Guard and Simplicia.

The rest continue offstage. He walks over to Simplicia and pokes her with his staff.

GENERAL
They've scraped the bottom of the barrel there.
he returns

KING
Bring that...that...thing to me.

The Guard does as he is told, bows, then exits. The King walks about Simplicia, the Queen holds her nose and the General pokes Simplicia with his staff.

KING
Your name?

SIMPLICIA
Simplicia.

GENERAL
giving her an extra hard poke
That's no name. Your name, the devil take you!

SIMPLICIA
crossing herself quickly, she looks for the devil
I can't see him.

KING
Can't see who?

SIMPLICIA
The devil.
she points at the General
Is that the devil?

KING
laughing
Where are you from, imp?

GENERAL
Who are you?

KING
Why are you dressed like that?

GENERAL
What's your name?

KING
Where are you from?

GENERAL
What are you?

KING
Where are you from?

GENERAL
Where are you from?

QUEEN
Stop it, you two. I want her, so get her cleaned up. What does a name matter?

KING
Yes, dear. General, you heard the Queen. Get it cleaned up, if it's possible.

He holds his nose and turns away. The King and Queen exit stage L.

GENERAL
Come on you.

He grabs Simplicia but finds the stink unbearable. He strides to the centre stage. Lights change to show an interior setting. Simplicia meekly follows. When she is beside the General he snaps his fingers.

GENERAL
Washers! Barber! Tailor!

MUSIC CUE 8

The Attendants enter and throughout the following scene the General beats in time with the music using his staff. The Attendants go about cleaning up Simplicia and changing her clothes (performed behind a screen). When they finish the Attendants stand back and allow the General to admire their work. Simplicia's new clothes are those of a court jester. The General nods his approval and the Attendants pay him for the privilege and depart stage L. Simplicia is very confused by all the events.

GENERAL
loudly, awakening Simplicia from her confusion
Don't forget I made you a page.

SIMPLICIA
A page? A page?

GENERAL
impatiently
A page! A page!

Two Attendants enter stage L. and place a long table upstage.

16

GENERAL
Put it in the centre, idiots.
they move it
to Simplicia
You wait on the King's table.

SIMPLICIA
Is that the table?

GENERAL
Yes, yes, yes!

SIMPLICIA
You want me to wait on the table?

GENERAL
Of course, fool. Now don't forget I made you a page. I'm
quite out of pocket by it.

SIMPLICIA
I'll get you another one.

GENERAL
turns on her, goes to hit her, then checks himself
Would you mind doing as you are told, please? The pigs
will be here soon.
he turns towards stage L. and yells
Food and drink.

The Attendants rush on with the food and drink and set the table.
It is soon prepared. The Attendants leave, paying the General as they
go. Simplicia climbs onto the table and stands in the centre. The
General turns and notices her.

GENERAL
What in the name of Thor are you doing there?

SIMPLICIA
innocently
You told me to wait. On the table.

GENERAL
Wait?

SIMPLICIA
For the pigs.

GENERAL
realising what is going on but not believing it
Get down stupid.
Simplicia gets down
Wait over there.

He points downstage R. Simplicia complies. As she passes, the General belts her with his staff. She yelps. Everything is now ready for the banquet.

The King and Queen plus their Guests (12) file in. The Guests are dressed in fancy costume depicting animals in the farmyard. They have masks on.* As they pass the table they take food and a goblet and then position themselves about the stage in appropriate positions, the King and Queen nearest the table. The meal and drinking progresses, quickly degenerating into an orgy, with everyone making a pig of themselves. Meanwhile Simplicia has been watching the whole scene but her eyes have been wandering as if she is looking for something. As the music progresses Simplicia begins to move about, searching. The King is satisfied so he stops eating. Music and Guests stop. Just at that moment Simplicia is looking under the table. The King grabs her and hauls her up. Music stops.

KING
What are you looking for?

SIMPLICIA
The pigs, sir.

KING
The pigs? The pigs? There are no pigs at the King's banquet.

GENERAL
embarrassed, shuffling forward
She's a bit...
taps his head
I'll fix it though.

KING
eyeing the General suspiciously
You do that.

GENERAL
pulling Simplicia away
Stand there so I can keep an eye on you.

*The purpose of the masks is to represent the Seven Deadly Sins - the General being Greed. The masks used in the original production were: Envy - snakes, Gluttony - pigs, Lust - cats, Pride - cock and hen, Sloth - fish, Anger - bull and cow. These masks are optional but care must be taken to use the animals referred to by Simplicia later in the script.

KING
calling out
Attendants, clear the table so my guests can dance.

MUSIC CUE 10

The orchestra 'tunes up'.   Attendants enter and clear the stage.

SIMPLICIA
frightened by the general activity
What are they going to do?

GENERAL
Dance.

SIMPLICIA
Dance?

GENERAL
Dance.

SIMPLICIA
What's dancing?

GENERAL
Well...
thinks
When the music starts they begin to jump up and down.

SIMPLICIA
Why do they do that?

GENERAL
thinks
So that the floor will fall through and collapse.

SIMPLICIA
But we'll all be killed.

GENERAL
Not if you use your head. When the dancing gets strongest
and the walls are about to go, the women grab the men so they
will have a soft landing.

MUSIC CUE 11

A vigorous dance follows. Simplicia is much too frightened to move.
The dance becomes more frantic and as it reaches its climax Simplicia
can stand it no longer and dashes straight to the King, grabs hold
of him and screams. The dance stops.

KING
angrily
What are you doing?

SIMPLICIA
Run for your lives. No, pray. Pray for deliverance.
notices nobody moving
Aren't you all frightened?

KING
Of what, you donkey?

SIMPLICIA
Of the destruction.

KING
Of the destruction?

SIMPLICIA
Of the...good gracious you're so brave!

KING
Brave?

SIMPLICIA
In the face of death.

KING
Death?

SIMPLICIA
When the walls and floor collapse.

KING
When the...

The King looks around him and notices a very embarrassed General.
He is suddenly aware of what is going on and bursts into a hearty
laugh. Everyone joins in.

KING
We have a ready-made fool here. Do we need a fool?

GUESTS
chorus
Yeeeeees!

KING
obviously annoyed with the General
You, get this donkey ready then and be quick about it.
calls
Wine while we wait.

GENERAL
to Simplicia
Come on you.

MUSIC CUE 12

*The General rushes Simplicia out before his already tenuous position
in the hierarchy worsens. They exit stage L. The Attendants re-enter
and serve the Guests wine. The Guests' conversation sounds like a
farmyard.
Simplicia re-enters. Music stops. Attendants depart. She is wearing
a donkey's head and tail. Her face is not covered. The guests stop
talking and watch Simplicia. Meanwhile she discovers her ears by
touch as she cannot see them. She notices her tail and spins about
the stage trying to catch it. She finally manages this feat by diving
between her legs and grabbing it. She falls over. The Guests laugh.
She gets up and stares. The Guests wait to see what she will do next.
Suddenly she brays at one of the Guests who backs away. The King
laughs. This relaxes everybody including Simplicia.*

SIMPLICIA
aside
Somehow I feel different. More confident. It must be the
costume. I wonder what I can get away with.

*Simplicia puts her head down and charges at the General who is sent
sprawling. She brays.*

KING
laughing
A fine donkey, General. Bring the donkey something to eat.

SIMPLICIA
Donkeys eat grass.
brays

KING
Not the King's donkey. She is special.

SIMPLICIA
Thank you, sir. I'll have cake.

KING
to the General
Cake for the donkey.
to Simplicia
How are you now, my donkey?

The General exits and returns with cake on a pottery bowl.

SIMPLICIA
Never felt better. Look, I've got a wet nose, and that's

21

a good sign. My hooves are in good condition and see how
my coat shines.
she takes the bowl from the General
What's this? A pottery bowl for the King's donkey?

KING
A gold bowl, General.

The General takes the bowl and exits.

SIMPLICIA
looking at the Guests then turning to the King
You've got some fine animals in this farmyard, sir.
going to one Guest
This is a nice looking heifer. Watch out for the old bull,
dear.

*The General returns with a gold plate and shoves it in Simplicia's
hand. She takes it and rubs herself against him.*

GENERAL
embarrassed
Watch it, you cheeky brat, or I'll have you thrown out.

*Simplicia brays as if in pain. The King gives the General a sharp
look. The Queen steps forward.*

QUEEN
sharply
General!

*Simplicia looks pleased with herself and dances about the stage, then
passes the plate to the General as if she didn't want it in the first
place. He passes it to a large woman dressed as a sow. Simplicia
notices this.*

SIMPLICIA
Are you the General's sow? We had a sow once. The General
seems to like pigs.
she moves to the other side of the stage, commenting as an aside
This is the first time a donkey has been head of a farmyard.
goes up to a man dressed as a cock
Hey feathers, your little henny wife has her eyes on a
younger rooster than you. He hasn't many feathers but he
can really crow.

The Guests laugh heartily. Simplicia goes up to the King.

SIMPLICIA
pointing at the General
Watch your dog, sir. Bones come easy from under your table.

The Guests laugh but a certain tension is evident as they begin to realise Simplicia is not so stupid. They are worried who will be next. Simplicia goes downstage away from the rest of the characters and begins her song. The Guests do not move throughout the song, remaining frozen until the verse is sung which applies to them. They animate for that particular section of the song which applies to the Sin they represent.

MUSIC CUE 13   THE FOOL'S SONG

SIMPLICIA
Once I dreamt the human race,
On the Tree of Life each had his place,
But now that dream reveals to me
Seven Sins hanging from that tree.

Pride it comes before a fall,
But they just don't seem to care at all.

Envy too is just as bad,
For they reach for the moon and it can't be had.

Then there's Lust, it's just a prop,
Always chasing, they never stop.

Anger's next, just look at them rage,
They fight over nothing, fight for an age.
Gluttony, eats like a pig,
He won't admit he's far too big.

Sloth is almost like the mule
Who won't even move to avoid a fool.

The General here is much the worst,
For his Greed for gold is such a curse.

If you've learnt the beat of this song,
Learn the words and you can't go wrong,
Can't go wrong, can't go wrong.

At the end of the song the Guests file out past the General, paying him gold as they go. As they go the General beats a constant rhythm on the ground with his staff. The King and Queen go last, not paying the General. Instead he bows as they pass.

TAPE CUE 4

As soon as they are gone there are sounds of a battle offstage.

*An alternative method of animating this song is for Simplicia to move towards each couple, representing each Sin, as she sings about it and the Guests to react to this.

*Frightened by the sound, the General drops his gold and runs
offstage. Simplicia, not understanding what is happening, runs
quickly and hides. Suddenly Edward, Olgard and a small troop of
Patriots race on the stage. Edward directs his men to search the
area and torch the tent. (Use similar lighting as at end of Scene 1.)
The troops go, and, satisfied there are no Barbarians about, Edward
leaves. Simplicia comes out of hiding and picks up the General's
gold. She then moves centre stage as the lights and tape fade. The
curtains close.*

----INTERVAL----

ACT II

SCENE 6   RETURN TO THE FOREST

*As the curtains open Simplicia is kneeling beside a grave with the Nun's
old Bible in her hand. She is dressed in the Nun's costume. On the
stage L. in the area used for the Nun's shelter in scene 3 there is
the donkey head and tail and the General's gold.
Once the lights are up full and the curtain is completely open,
Edward creeps on stage and stands behind Simplicia. She is unaware
anyone is there. Music ends.
During the next section of dialogue Edward signals offstage and
Olgard and the rest of Edward's troops enter silently. Edward
signals Olgard to go to the hut, which he does. He returns with
the costume and the gold.
Simplicia is completely unaware of what is going on as she speaks.*

SIMPLICIA
Oh Sister, I have been here two years now and still you
have not answered my prayers...Who am I?...What am I?...
What is it God has destined me to do?

*She bows her head. Suddenly the grave is lit by a strong light.
Simplicia looks up, startled. She appears to be listening in between
the snatches of what she says.*

SIMPLICIA
...But how can I, a mere girl, hope to achieve such an
important task?...how do I find such people?...Yes, Sister,
God's will be done.

*Begin music cue before opening curtains.

At this point the light goes and Simplicia is taken prisoner by Edward's troops. They take her offstage R. She carries the Bible with her.

SIMPLICIA
crying out as she goes
Sister, Sister, look out for me as my task has begun.

TAPE CUE 5

NUN'S VOICE
off stage
Find thyself and be true, Simplicia.

The lights fade

SCENE 7   THE PATRIOT CAMP: ON TRIAL

MUSIC CUE 15

As the lights come up, the Patriots enter from both sides of the stage and line up. Two Throne Guards carry on the throne and place it centre stage. They stand behind the throne. The Patriot Officer enters bearing a tray holding a Gold Cup (of chalice size) and stands downstage L. Simplicia is brought on between two Patriot soldiers and stands to the R. of the throne. She carries the Bible and is still dressed in the Nun's costume. The music ends.

PATRIOT OFFICER
Pray cheer for our illustrious leader.

MUSIC CUE 16

PATRIOTS
cheering
Edmund!

Edmund, old and dignified, enters. He is flanked by his son, Edward. Edmund moves to the throne, the Patriot Officer steps forward with the tray, Edmund takes the Gold Cup, lifts it upwards and drinks from it. Edward stands to the R. of the throne.

EDMUND
holding the Cup high
Oh God, help me to temper justice with mercy as you have done. Give me the wisdom of Solomon so that I might know what should be done with this strange girl my son captured in the forest.

Edmund replaces the Cup on the tray and sits on the throne. The Officer returns to his place.

EDMUND
to Edward
Tell me, son, how you found this girl.

EDWARD
Well, father, we were behind the enemy camp, in the Forest
of Hanaven, when we came across this old hut. Inside the
hut we found gold, lots of it. Enemy gold. We also found
this.

*He signals offstage. Olgard enters holding up the donkey's head
and tail. He begins to act the fool with it. Laughter.*

EDWARD
signalling quiet
Go on.

Olgard exits then re-enters having discarded the costume.

EDWARD
We looked around and noticed the girl. She was on her
knees beside a tatty old grave, but she did not seem to
be praying.

EDMUND
What was she doing, then?

EDWARD
The grave seemed to be lit up through a clearing in the
trees...the sun I suppose...and she was...well...just
staring up at this light.

EDMUND
I see. Go on.

EDWARD
We captured the girl and questioned her. She said the
donkey's head was hers when she was a fool.
laughter
The gold had been stolen by a Barbarian General and she
was looking after it till her sister told her what it
should be used for.
laughter
And that's the story, father.

EDMUND
That helps a lot.
to Simplicia, kindly
Come here, girl, I won't bite.
she steps forward, apparently unafraid
Is what my son tells me the truth, girl?

SIMPLICIA
Yes, sir.

EDMUND
You don't deny it?

SIMPLICIA
No, sir. A son doesn't lie to his father.

EDMUND
Mine does, if it suits him.
laughter. Edward looks embarrassed

SIMPLICIA
You should not say such sinful things about your son, sir.

EDMUND
A minx! You have captured a minx, Edward. Aren't you
scared of me, girl?

SIMPLICIA
Yes, sir. For you are powerful and strong and brave. I
am only a girl...and a fool. But if I were to show my fear
you would not listen to the important things I have been
sent to tell you.

EDMUND
sternly
Sent? You were captured.

SIMPLICIA
Only because my Sister meant it to be.

EDMUND
with a hint of sarcasm
You must have a kind sister.

SIMPLICIA
seriously
The kindest of all, sir.

EDMUND
softening a little
Tell me your name, girl.

SIMPLICIA
Simplicia, sir.

EDMUND
And who gave you such a name, Simplicia?

SIMPLICIA
My Sister, sir.

EDMUND
Is she older than you?

SIMPLICIA
Oh yes, sir, about your age.

EDMUND
Your parents must be old then?

SIMPLICIA
Yes, sir, about your age. But they're dead now.

EDMUND
Your parents are dead and your sister looks after you.

SIMPLICIA
My parents and Ursula were killed by wolves.

EDMUND
By wolves? And who is Ursula?

SIMPLICIA
Ursula was my sister, sir...and my Sister told me they
were Barbarians.

EDMUND
Where do the Barbarians enter the story?

SIMPLICIA
They were the wolves, sir.

EDMUND
almost in despair
Your parents and sister were killed by wolves who were
Barbarians and you were looked after by your sister?

SIMPLICIA
Yes sir.

EDMUND
And what happened next?

SIMPLICIA
seriously
I became a fool, sir.

There is raucous laughter. Simplicia looks hurt and confused.
Edmund almost gives up in despair, then quietens the troops.

EDMUND
Shall we start again? Simplicia, where are you from?

SIMPLICIA
Hanaven, sir. I minded my father's animals. One day the
Barbarians came and killed all my family.

EDMUND
You said wolves.

SIMPLICIA
At the time I thought they were, sir.

EDMUND
beginning to understand
Go on.

SIMPLICIA
I escaped into the forest where an old nun rescued me.

EDMUND
Whom you call your sister?

SIMPLICIA
Yes, sir...She taught me about God and that I must learn
to be myself.

EDMUND
Yourself?

SIMPLICIA
Yes, sir, and then she died. I was captured by the
Barbarians and became a fool for the King.

EDMUND
understanding
Hence the costume.

SIMPLICIA
going on
Our troops attacked and I escaped with the General's gold
and returned to the forest.

EDMUND
Our troops? Don't you mean my troops?

SIMPLICIA
Yes, sir, my troops.

EDMUND
a little sarcastically
Your troops?

SIMPLICIA
And yours, sir.
laughter

EDMUND
growing in impatience
Go on, please.

SIMPLICIA
I lived in the forest for another two years till my Sister
told me to find her brother and help him to drive the
Barbarians from our land so peace could once again return.
Your son was sent to find me.

EDMUND
The Nun, who is dead, told you to find her brother and
fight the Barbarians.

SIMPLICIA
Yes, sir, God let her return to me.

*The troops cry 'blasphemy'. Edmund, whose patience is almost gone,
quietens them. He is sure this girl is trying to make a fool of him.*

EDMUND
angrily
You tell me some fantastic story and expect me to believe
it. Have you any proof?

SIMPLICIA
Yes, sir, in this book.

*She steps forward and hands the Bible to Edmund. He opens the front
cover and turns pale.*

EDMUND
reading
"Simplicia, keep these holy words close to your heart so
that you might understand yourself."
he closes the book and stands
I know this writing. It belongs to my sister who became a
Child of God many years ago.
the troops react to this revelation
She left the convent to become a hermit until the war was
over. Now she is dead but the war continues.

He looks at Simplicia. There are tears in his eyes. He embraces her.

EDMUND
You were her daughter, from now you will be mine.

*During the song Edmund hands Simplicia the Cup. She drinks from it.
Then Edmund and Edward embrace her in turn.*

MUSIC CUE 17   THE PATRIOTS' ANTHEM

PATRIOTS
Proud of her people I love my country,
And as I fight for her freedom I know God will go with me,
Through hate and death and sacrifice His glory I shall see.

See your proud country, we must set her free,
So we must all pray to God to help us end this tyranny,
To bring us back to life again in peace and harmony.

God guard us, guide us, grant us liberty,
And send us out to do Thy bidding now in all sincerity,
That we may live to praise Thy name, to love and honour Thee,

That we may live to love again.

At the end of the song the troops depart in an orderly fashion.
They cheer Simplicia as they go. Edmund, Edward and Simplicia depart,
arm in arm, stage R. The Throne Guards remove the throne and the
Officer removes the Cup. The lights fade.

SCENE 8   THE PATRIOT CAMP: LOVE AND DEATH

Sounds of laughter and sword play are heard offstage as the lights
come up.* *Simplicia darts on stage from the R., sword in hand. She*
is dressed in a Patriot outfit which should include green.** *She*
taunts her opponent playfully. Edward follows trying to keep pace
with her but failing. He is obviously tired.

EDWARD
stopping, leaning on his sword, trying to catch his breath
Enough...you are...wearing me out...I don't...understand
...In two months...you have become...the best fighter...
in the camp.

SIMPLICIA
cheerful, teasing
Come on, old man, you are supposed to be teaching me to
fight.

EDWARD
recovering
Let's call it a day. I'm tired.

*Time is needed for Simplicia to change costume - hence
the laughter cue.
**Although the choice of colour for the Patriots is optional,
Simplicia needs some green because of the line in the Ballad
(Scene 9).

SIMPLICIA
turning away in mock disgust
Men are all the same. Talk big, but when it comes to
action "not today, I'm too tired."

Edward reacts to this comment by attacking Simplicia from behind.

EDWARD
in full flight
We'll see who's tired.

*Simplicia reacts to this renewed attack just in time. A sword fight
follows which uses the whole stage. Simplicia gradually gains control.
Suddenly Edward gets a little too close in a bid to regain control.
Simplicia's sword, instead of connecting with his, nicks Edward's
wrist. Edward drops his sword and lets out a cry of pain. Simplicia
immediately drops her sword and rushes to help him. She takes his
wrist, takes a piece of binding from her costume and begins to wrap
the cut. Edward kisses her playfully. Simplicia backs away, not
knowing how to react. She becomes very coy and shy. Edward steps
forward and gently takes her hands in his. Simplicia moves downstage
L. and Edward remains centre stage for the song. Simplicia returns
to the centre at the end of the song.*

MUSIC CUE 18* LOVE DUET

EDWARD
Why is it you never talk to me?
Why is it I cannot make you see?
I've tried, but I just can't explain,
I'm in love, but all I feel is pain.

Why is it you always run from me?
Why is it you want to stay so free?
I've tried, but can no more restrain,
I'm in love, but all you bring is pain.

Why is it you never talk to me?
Why is it you always run from me?
Talk to me, talk to me.

SIMPLICIA
But I have never known this thing you call love,
It's hard for me to understand,
My heart still lies with those who guide from above,
So give me time to know my mind,
Perhaps one day I'll give my hand.

EDWARD
Why can't you admit your love for me?

*Alternative version (18A) if Edward is played by a boy.

32

Why can't you see clearly destiny?
I'm tired, I can't sleep anymore,
I'm confused, what are these feelings for?

Why can't you admit your love for me?
Why can't you see clearly destiny?

Destiny,
Please...love...me.

At the end of the song, Simplicia kisses Edward gently on the forehead.

SIMPLICIA
gently
You are sweet, Edward, and I like you a lot.

EDWARD
Like, but not love. Simplicia, you are a beautiful child.

SIMPLICIA
And you, Edward, are my teacher.

EDWARD
I will always love you, Simplicia, even if only from afar.
I wish you could be mine and pray one day it will happen.

He picks up his sword and departs sadly stage L. Simplicia turns towards him as he goes, then picks up her sword and looks skywards. She is almost in tears.

SIMPLICIA
Oh Sister, please make me understand this thing Edward calls love.

MUSIC CUE 19

Simplicia departs stage L. The following action should follow the music cue. The lights cross fade to give a shadowy effect (night-time?). Edmund enters upstage R. He is carrying the Gold Cup. He looks thoughtful. He moves downstage L. and holds the Cup skywards appearing to pray.
Three Raiders appear upstage L. in the shadows. They close in on Edmund and stab him to death. As he collapses one of them take the Gold Cup. The Raiders quickly and quietly depart. The lights brighten a little. Edward and his friends enter stage L. They notice the body. Edward rushes to the body while Olgard leaves the stage. The others join Edward. Having seen there is nothing he can do Edward moves to the R. of the stage - alone in his sorrow. Funeral music begins. Olgard enters with Simplicia who assumes control by gently crossing Edmund's arms across his breast. Simplicia stands, looks towards Edward, realises he wishes to be alone and departs.

33

The remaining Patriots step back to form a guard of honour. Edward
returns to the body, kisses it goodbye, then makes the following
speech. Music ends.

EDWARD
Father, the bitterness of war has finally touched my heart.
I begin to understand the feelings of the peasants we have
rallied to our cause. For them it is a fight to be free,
for me it has been a game of heroics. I, too, must sacrifice
if this land of ours is ever to be free of the Barbarians.
I will leave Simplicia, leave this haven until your death
is avenged and peace once again restored.

Edward makes the sign of the cross and departs stage R. The others
follow him at a discreet distance. Lights fade.

SCENE 9   THE PATRIOT CAMP: EXPLOITS OF A WOLF

The Patriot soldiers and a group of camp followers enter and arrange
themselves about the stage in various groups. Each group is involved
in something different, e.g. cooking, cleaning weapons, chatting-up
a camp follower, etc. There should be an air of business about the
place. (Edmund departs under cover of all this action).
When the scene is ready the lights come up.
Downstage centre stand a group of three Patriots and Ellen, a camp
*follower. To the left is Aidan, cleaning his lute**

1st PATRIOT
slapping Ellen's backside
It's a pity you're not more like the Wolf.

ELLEN
rubbing her backside
Hey!...Who's this wolf, anyway?

2nd PATRIOT
A raider of the night. A creature who is tearing the enemy
apart. Simplicia.

ELLEN
a hurtful look on her face
She's not perfect you know. There are things I can do that
she can't.
laughter

3rd PATRIOT
If there were more of us like her, we wouldn't have time

*Aidan can use a guitar instead of a lute, and accompany
himself (herself) on stage.

for what you can do.

1st PATRIOT
Everywhere she goes the Barbarians are beaten.

2nd PATRIOT
Did you hear how she fooled the King's own personal
bodyguard?

1st PATRIOT
You mean when they had her trapped?

2nd PATRIOT
Yes.

ELLEN
interested
What happened?

1st PATRIOT
Well the enemy had her surrounded, see. There was no
escape. Her followers wanted to fight it out but they were
outnumbered. So the Wolf had them climb on a nearby roof
and make plenty of noise. Meanwhile she smeared her face
in dirt and leapt at their leader with a blazing torch. It
was dark and the Barbarians were sure it was the wrath of
Woden.

The three Patriots burst into laughter. Ellen's respect for
Simplicia is growing.

ELLEN
exasperated
Well, what happened next?

2nd PATRIOT
in between his own laughter
They turned heel...and ran...left their weapons...and food
behind. Kept us fed for a week.

3rd PATRIOT
Hey, Aidan, give us one of your songs.

1st PATRIOT
A song. A song about the Wolf.

Aidan steps forward to sing. As he does so he strums the opening
bars. The rest of the Patriots stop what they are doing to listen.

MUSIC CUE 20   THE BALLAD OF SIMPLICIA

AIDAN
Our country held in trouble and war
Was being torn apart,
When from the dark a maiden fair
Uplifted all our hearts.

PATRIOTS
A wolf in human form,
Inspired by God alone.

AIDAN
She's dressed so fine in huntsman green,
She wanders far and wide,
No enemy does dare to meet
The scourge of the countryside.

PATRIOTS
A wolf in human form,
Inspired by God alone.

AIDAN
She leads her troops on many a raid
Into our land defiled,
Spreading hope where'er she goes,
With the innocence of a child.

PATRIOTS
A wolf in human form,
Inspired by God alone.

AIDAN
And though the war is far from won,
Her love begins to grow,
To search for Edward long since lost,
The Wolf she has to go.

PATRIOTS
A wolf in human form,
Inspired by God alone, God alone, God alone.

*At the end of the song the Patriots and camp followers leave the
stage taking all their gear with them. Ellen remains behind and
watches them depart - slightly annoyed.*

ELLEN
Men! They love you and leave you. Their heart is somewhere
else. But I'll show them! And another woman will help me.
It's the only sex you can trust.

Ellen exits determinedly. The lights fade.

36

SCENE 10   THE GENERAL'S CAMP: RETURN OF THE GOLD CUP

*As the lights come up the General is seated on a chair centre stage.
It is the inside of his tent. Beside him is a pedestal with the
Gold Cup on top. At the back of the stage on either side of the area
designated for the tent stand two guards. The General's foot is
heavily bandaged. He is puffy faced and very red. He is suffering
from gout. He stands using his staff for support.*

GENERAL
Owww! I'm in pain. Attendant, quickly.
no reply
louder
Attendant!

The Attendant enters

ATTENDANT
Yes, sir.

GENERAL
Can't you see I'm in pain? The plague of some devil is
upon me...I'm dying...
he puts his foot down
...Owww!

ATTENDANT
Im very sorry, sir.

GENERAL
Sorry, sorry. You're sorry! Don't stand there being
sorry. Do something about it.

ATTENDANT
cowering
I don't know what I can do, sir.

GENERAL
Well being sorry isn't going to help...
he goes to hit the Attendant with his staff
...Owww!

ATTENDANT
Why don't you sit down, sir. I'll call Cassandra. Maybe
she has a solution.

GENERAL
That old sorceress. I hate her solutions. They taste
foul.

he moves
Ohwww!...Don't stand there. Get her. Get her now!

The Attendant departs quickly. The General sits.

GENERAL
A plague on this country and its peasantry. Ever since
that stupid girl stated raving about some lunatic god
and the right of every imbecile that ever walked to have
freedom and land, this country has gone potty.

Andrea creeps on stage L., stabs and removes the nearest bodyguard.

GENERAL
I don't know. The food is poisonous. The wine tastes
like ratsbane. My men act like sheep every time the word
'wolf' is mentioned.

*Ellen, now dressed as one of Simplicia's followers, creeps on and
removes the other bodyguard.*

GENERAL
Wolf...Wolf...and her pack of she-devils - just five
minutes alone with her is all I want. Even with this
fetid leg...
he belts it with his staff
Owww! Where is that hag? Any venom is better than this...
Attendant!...Cassandra!!!

*An old woman dressed in a cloak and mask, covered in talismans and
magic charms, comes on stage. The fact that it is Simplicia in
disguise should not be obvious to the audience, nor, of course, to
the General.*

GENERAL
Oh there you are.

SIMPLICIA
in the voice of an old woman
You called, General?

GENERAL
sarcastically
No, no, dear, I was just exercising my lungs.
shouting
Of course I called, you silly old bag of bones. Do something
about my leg.

SIMPLICIA
Now, now, General, tantrums never cured anything.
Cassandra will fix her General's leg.

GENERAL
a little calmer
I hope it works this time.

Simplicia hands the General a bottle of potion from under her cloak.

SIMPLICIA
Here, General, try this. Just a mouthful and you'll soon
be well again.

GENERAL
taking the bottle
Are you sure it will work?

SIMPLICIA
Trust me, sir, and things will soon be put right.

*The General takes a swig and immediately spits it out. At the same
time he puts too much pressure on his foot.*

GENERAL
OWWW! You old hag, you tried to poison me.

SIMPLICIA
Calm down, General. It is clear you don't like my
medicine. Well old Cassandra has one idea left. I will
cast a spell which will disperse your misery...

GENERAL
interrupting
A spell! A Barbarian General resorting to hocus pocus!
We're civilised now, you know.

SIMPLICIA
Sometimes the ancient ways are best.

GENERAL
Well alright. But don't tell anyone, mind, or I'll have
your head. I'm a big enough laughing stock as it is.

SIMPLICIA
Just trust me, General.

TAPE CUE 6

*Simplicia takes a charm from around her neck and places it around
the General's neck. Then she starts a witch's chant. Lights fade
a little.*

SIMPLICIA
"Hubble, bubble, toil and trouble
I call on Isis and her double

I call on Rocasta and her friends
Once again to make amends
For the cruelty of the gods
Issued out to men with faults
Make his load a great deal lighter
Make his future that much brighter
Please, O friends, do not fail
There's a sting in the Wolf's tail."

*Tape fades and lights return to original position before the last
line. On the last line Simplicia discards her cloak and mask to
reveal who she is.*

GENERAL
What the...
recovering quickly
Guards! Guards!

SIMPLICIA
I asked them to leave us alone.

GENERAL
regaining his composure
So you're the mighty Wolf? You look more like a scarecrow
to me.

SIMPLICIA
You don't recognise me, do you General?

GENERAL
Should I? I assume this pathetic creature I see in front
of me is the infamous Wolf?

SIMPLICIA
More than that, General.

GENERAL
More than a scavenger who often robs me of my supplies?

SIMPLICIA
You're fat enough. But, General, surely you recognise a
good fool?

GENERAL
Any creature who steps inside this tent is a fool.

SIMPLICIA
Well said, General, but you still don't recognise me, do
you?

GENERAL
Until I've had my breakfast I wouldn't recognise my own
mother.

SIMPLICIA
calling offstage
Godwin, bring the General his breakfast.

Godwin enters carrying a plate holding the donkey's head and tail.

SIMPLICIA
For you, General.

GENERAL
suddenly recognising Simplicia
You!
quickly recovering from his initial shock
A donkey!
laughs
My men are frightened of a donkey! The Wolf who raids the
countryside is a donkey!

SIMPLICIA
You raid, General, I protect.

*The General brings up his staff to hit Simplicia. She is quicker
and knocks it from his hand with her sword. The General falls, hurting
his leg.*

GENERAL
Owww! Damn this leg! Damn you!

SIMPLICIA
Now, now, General, we mustn't be a sore loser.

GENERAL
struggles to his feet, Simplicia hands him his staff
What is it you want from me?

SIMPLICIA
The return of the Gold Cup and vengeance for the death of
Edmund.

GENERAL
Get it over with. Kill me, then. Anything is better than
this leg.

SIMPLICIA
Kill you, my friend? I owe you too much for that, dear
General. That shall be Edward's pleasure, if he so chooses.
to Godwin
Call the others. The General is waiting.

GODWIN
calling offstage
Andrea, Ellen, don't keep the General waiting.

*Andrea and Ellen enter. They hold the General while Godwin dresses
him in the head and tail.*

MUSIC CUE 21

*Simplicia takes the staff and bangs the floor with it in time to the
music. The General, once he is dressed, looks bewildered and begins
to explore his costume. He limps about in a circle chasing his tail.
Failing to catch it he bends between his legs and grabs it. He falls
over. The Patriots laugh. Music ends.*

SIMPLICIA
A fine fool!

GODWIN
A fine fool indeed!

ELLEN
A typical male!

*The lights dim a little. Simplicia takes the Cup and she and her
followers exit. The General limps to downstage centre to sing.*

MUSIC CUE 22   THE GENERAL'S SONG

GENERAL
Who is the fool now?
Who is the fool now?
I've done some bad things,
But I'll change somehow.

This donkey's lost now,
I need a cross now,
I want to believe in Him,
To Him I'll bow.

Who is the fool now?
Who is the fool now?
The fool is me.

The General exits. The lights fade.

SCENE 11   THE PATRIOT CAMP: FINAL PREPARATIONS

The lights come up.

MUSIC CUE 23   GLORIA

*The Patriot soldiers enter from both sides of the stage singing
'Gloria' and line up on both sides of the stage leaving a space down
the middle. The Officer enters and moves downstage L. carrying the*

Gold Cup on a tray. Before the end of the 'Gloria' Simplicia,
flanked by Godwin, Andrea and Ellen, enters. They move towards the
front of the stage.

SIMPLICIA
to Godwin
There seems to be a good number here. Did nobody take the
opportunity to leave?

GODWIN
No, Simplicia. In fact our numbers have increased since
the word got round that you would be leading them into
battle.

SIMPLICIA
They are brave men and women, for many will die.

GODWIN
Brave, my lady? They would follow the Wolf anywhere for
they trust you.

SIMPLICIA
I hope I do not betray that trust.

GODWIN
There is no chance of that. Besides you have God on your
side.

SIMPLICIA
And He will save us from destruction, aye Godwin?

GODWIN
So you have always said and the troops believe you.

SIMPLICIA
a slight note of doubt
So be it.
to Andrea
How are your daughters, Andrea?

ANDREA
With you, Simplicia.

SIMPLICIA
to Ellen
And how do you feel, Ellen?

ELLEN
Like leaving now.

SIMPLICIA
Scared?

43

ELLEN
Yes. But I'll stay. You can't settle down and have a
family with Barbarians about.

SIMPLICIA
No, that's true.

Simplicia and Godwin should now talk to one or two of the Patriots,
Godwin appearing the more formal. Although she is clearly the
accepted leader, Simplicia should not appear unapproachable. The way
this is conveyed will depend on staging. Simplicia moves centre
stage for the following speech.

SIMPLICIA
For twenty years the war has raged about us, unabating and
merciless. For twenty years we have seen force met with
force, men and women, peasants and armies perish, and the
stink of death has been forever in our noses. Imagine, my
brothers and sisters in God, if that were to be all over
and you could once again return to your land, free to till
your soil, free to openly speak your language, free to
practise your faith without fear. That, my friends, is
God's promise to you if you follow me today.
Edward has driven the Barbarians to within two days march
from here. In the forests surrounding Hanaven. The Gold
Cup is returned. Many of their leaders are dead or gone.
They outnumber us but together we can overcome their armies
and the land of our forefathers will once again be at peace.
Some of us will die, but our descendants will remember.
Some of us will live and our descendants will remember and
they will proudly say of us - my father, my mother fought
at Hanaven and saved the day.
My friends, To Arms for Hanaven!

PATRIOTS
To Arms for Simplicia! To Arms for the Wolf!

The Officer moves to centre stage with the Cup. Simplicia takes it
and holds it aloft, then returns it to the tray. During the song
Simplicia, Godwin, Andrea and Ellen move into the background. The
Officer returns to his position.

MUSIC CUE 24   THE PATRIOTS' ANTHEM

PATRIOTS
Proud of her people I love my country,
And as I fight for her freedom I know God will go with me,
Through hate and death and sacrifice His glory I shall see.

See your proud country, we must set her free,
So we must all pray to God to help us end this tyranny,
To bring us back to life again in peace and harmony.

God guard us, guide us, grant us liberty,
And send us out to do Thy bidding now in all sincerity,
That we may live to praise Thy name, to love and honour Thee,

That we may live to love again.

At the end of the song the Patriots exit R. to the accompaniment of
a repeat of part of the Anthem. Simplicia, Godwin et al. exit. The
Officer goes last. The lights fade.

SCENE 12   THE BATTLE OF HANAVEN: FINALE

The lights come up. The scene should be very shadowy at the opening
of the scene.

TAPE CUE 7

The Tape should play right through the scene until the entrance of
Simplicia. At the start of the scene the stage is bare. After a
few seconds Edward and Olgard enter from the L. Olgard is wounded.
Edward is tired and looking worried.

EDWARD
shouting above the din
The battle goes badly, dear friend.

OLGARD
And will get worse. We have few men left and the Barbarians
seem to be coming from everywhere.

EDWARD
At least Simplicia has recovered the Cup and avenged my
father's death.

OLGARD
And you, Edward, have made it possible for Simplicia to
arrive with reinforcements.

EDWARD
It may be too late.

A Messenger enters from the R. and approaches Edward.

EDWARD
Good day messenger, what news of Simplicia?

MESSENGER
She is not two hours march away and she brings thousands.

EDWARD
Return, good messenger, and tell her to hurry. We are
almost lost.

MESSENGER
I shall do your bidding, sir.
he exits stage R.

EDWARD
to nobody in particular
Simplicia - she is my one regret.

OLGARD
Regret, sir? Surely not. For without her...

EDWARD
Oh, not the way you mean. My regret is I will never see
her again.

OLGARD
I see.

EDWARD
Do you? Yes I believe you do.

A Patriot enters from stage L.

PATRIOT
Sir, sir, the Barbarians have broken through. All is lost.

EDWARD
recovering his composure
Lost? Lost? With Simplicia on her way? The battle is not
yet done.
to Olgard
Come, let us show these wolves what men are made of.

*They exit stage R. The tape gets louder and lighting effects should
convey the atmosphere of battle. About 2 minutes of separate battle
scenes should take place. These should develop out of improvisation
and are more effective if stylised. At first it appears as though
the Barbarians might be winning but it soon swings in Simplicia's
favour with the tendency of the movement from R. to L.**
*At the end of these skirmishes the tape fades and the cry of 'Victory'
is heard off stage. The lights brighten and Simplicia, Godwin and
Andrea enter from stage R.*

*In the original production the following series of
skirmishes was used.
1.   A group of Patriot bowmen enter from the R. and fire a
     round towards the L.
2.   A charge from L. to R. by a group of Barbarians
     brandishing axes.
3.   A group of Patriot spearmen enter from the R. and move
     downstage then charge off stage L. in search of Barbarians.
4.   Two wounded Barbarians enter from the L. and are taken
     prisoner by Patriots entering from the R.
5.   'Victory'

GODWIN
They are beaten, Simplicia. We have won a fair victory.

SIMPLICIA
And lost.

ANDREA
taken aback
And lost, Simplicia, how can that be?

SIMPLICIA
Many good men and women have been killed on both sides,
and for what?

ANDREA
For freedom.

SIMPLICIA
with a touch of bitterness
And pride. Patriotism, my friends, has cost us all a high
price. Even Ellen and your daughters, Andrea. Edward too.
I only hope it was worth it.

*Simplicia moves further downstage. She is close to tears. As she
makes the following statement the armies, the Patriots and Barbarians,
enter and fill the stage.*

SIMPLICIA
looking heavenwards
Oh Sister, I have done as you commanded and you rob me of
my reward. Why, Sister? Why, God? Have I not done all
that you wished? Have I not helped drive the Barbarians
from our land? Then why must I be left alone?

*She bows her head. Meanwhile the Officer bearing the Cup approaches
Simplicia and hands the Cup towards her.*

OFFICER
You are not alone, Simplicia, you are with us. In
recognition of your noble deeds we feel this rightly belongs
to you.

*Simplicia turns towards the armies and turns back to the Cup. She
looks at it.*

OFFICER
All hail Simplicia! All hail our new Queen!

*Simplicia takes the Cup and holds it up. She begins to draw it
towards her lips but does not drink. Instead she returns it to the
tray.*

SIMPLICIA
No, it is not meant for me. My task is complete. I am a
soldier. Peacetime is for politicians and diplomats, not
soldiers. May they not fail in their duty as we have not.
Friends, return to your land for peasants are the most noble
of God's creatures. I must go to Edward for I know he
cannot be dead.

*Simplicia departs stage L. The soldiers gather about the front of
the stage leaving a space down the centre.*

MUSIC CUE 25   THE FINALE

SOLDIERS (i.e. PATRIOTS & BARBARIANS)
Now, now we are free,
Onward we go, the battle has been won.
Now, safe home again,
Onward we go, our work has now just begun.

Tend to your land,
Come everyone,
Think anew,
Heal the wounds,
Take the plough,
Sow your seed,
And give praises to God.

Now, now we are free,
Onward we go, the battle has been won.
Now, safe home again,
Onward we go, our work has now just begun.

Put down your swords,
Come everyone,
Lend a hand,
Hide the scars,
Build new towns,
We must plan,
And give praises to God.

Now, now we are free,
Onward we go, the battle has been won.
Now, safe home again,
Our work has just begun.

*Edward and Simplicia enter stage L. and come down the centre to the
front.*

EDWARD AND SIMPLICIA
We're united in love,
Together again,
And fate's played its hand from the start.

48

The remainder of the cast now enter and join the others.

WHOLE CAST
United in love,
Together again,
And fate's played its hand from the start.

Oh Simplicia, lead the way for us,
Oh Simplicia, won't you pray for us?
Oh Simplicia, you will be our guiding light.

Oh Simplicia, bless our land for us,
Oh Simplicia, guard our towns for us,
Oh Simplicia, you will be our guiding light.

CHORUS STAGE RIGHT
Now the future is laid before us,
And we have dreams which are filled with promises,

CHORUS STAGE LEFT
Now a better life stretches before us,

WHOLE CAST
And we believe in the bright day that's just begun.

Oh Simplicia, lead the way for us,
Oh Simplicia, won't you pray for us?
Oh Simplicia, you will be our guiding light.

Oh Simplicia, bless our land for us,
Oh Simplicia, guard our towns for us,
Oh Simplicia, you will be our guiding light,
Our Guiding Light.

(CURTAIN)

THE   END